DISSOLVE

ALSO BY SHERWIN BITSUI

Flood Song
Shapeshift

Dissolve

SHERWIN BITSUI

COPPER CANYON PRESS

Port Townsend, Washington

Cover art: Reuben Wu, *Lux Noctis: Bisti Badlands I*

Copper Canyon Press is in residence at Fort Worden State Park in Port Townsend, Washington, under the auspices of Centrum. Centrum is a gathering place for artists and creative thinkers from around the world, students of all ages and backgrounds, and audiences seeking extraordinary cultural enrichment.

LIBRARY OF CONGRESS CATALOGING-IN-PUBLICATION DATA

Names: Bitsui, Sherwin, 1975– author.
Title: Dissolve / Sherwin Bitsui.
Description: Port Townsend, Washington : Copper Canyon Press, [2018]
Identifiers: LCCN 2018016188 | ISBN 9781556595455 (pbk. : alk. paper)
Subjects: LCSH: Navajo Indians—Poetry.
Classification: LCC PS3602.I85 A6 2018 | DDC 811/.6—dc23
LC record available at https://lccn.loc.gov/2018016188

9 8 7 6 5 4 3 2 FIRST PRINTING

Copper Canyon Press
Post Office Box 271
Port Townsend, Washington 98368

www.coppercanyonpress.org

For shi naalí Louise Bitsue

CONTENTS

DISSOLVE

The Caravan

The city's neon embers
stripe the asphalt's blank page
where this story pens itself nightly,
where ghosts weave their oily hair
into his belt of ice,
dress him in pleated shadows
and lay him fetal
on the icy concrete—
the afterbirth of sirens glistening over him.

We drain our headlights
on his scraped forehead
and watch the December moon
two-step across his waxen eyes;
his mouth's shallow pond—
      a reflecting pool
         where his sobs leak into my collar.

One more, just one more, he whispers,
as he thaws back into the shape of *nihitsilí,*
bruised knees thorning against his chest.

We steal away,
our wheels moan
through sleet and ash.

Death places second, third,
and fourth behind us.

At home on the Reservation:
Father sifts dried cedar leaves
over glowing embers;
Mother, hovering

above cellphone light, awaits:
> *He's okay,*
> *never went out,*
> *watched a movie instead.*

But tonight,
my speech has knives
that quiver at the ellipses
of neon Budweiser signs
blinking through the fogged windshield,
and I text:
> I've only rescued a sliver of him,
> he's only twenty-five
> and he smells like blood and piss,
> his turquoise bracelet snatched for pawn,
> by the same ghost who traded his jacket
> for a robe of snow and ice,
> before inviting him
> back into the Caravan
>> for *one more, just one more.*

Dissolve

On limbs of slanted light
painted with my mind's skin color,
I step upon black braids,
oil-drenched, worming
from last month's orphaned mouth.

Winged with burning—
I ferry them
        from my filmed eyes, wheezing.

Scalp blood in my footprints—
my buckskin pouch filling
        with photographed sand.

No language but its rind
        crackling in the past tense.

This poem pivots a walking cane,
then sniffs vacuum-packed air
strung from pawnshop windows;
it climbs cloud hair
only to fall back upon red soil—
saltwater masks sweating
          on our smeared faces.

Unbelted from snow-dusted fog,
night-stretching-out-longer-than-anticipated
abalones the waking that creaks
          when soaked in the blood of dragonflies.

Hunched over the sleeping,
this night wears
a garden's dust cloud,
cleaves body heat
from a barometer with pine claws.

Its head, gaseous in hindsight,
grows a third shadow,
drifts past fog-rimmed children's wails,
then licks dry—
rain-moistened teeth
        steaming in plastic bags.

Hammering liquid night
to the lake's final skeleton,
our sawtoothed tailbones tingle
in the mirror we changed our minds in.

Strangers to our breath,
we wheeze in dying trees
then take the shape
of toothless mouths suckling
the driest month's driest branches.

Coaxed over a barbed fence-line,
strummed into cricket chirp,
this address wears the fog's yellow ankles
toward the floor plan
of a reservation spiraling
back from the aftermath,
        dust-dappled mist in its craw,
        engine fluid trailing its gullet.

An elegy hands me a busy signal.

Its handle broke me from my tooth.

I chew its answers
    until I taste cracks
    in the chrome
        outline of a sky   (without hands).

Notice: every link in the trail to *here*

      is a bullet's path   to *back there.*

The hue of off-color messages: *collapsed.*

What crows above a city's em dash,
doused in whale oil,
        hangs here—named: *nameless.*

Covering its sobs with corral dirt,
I imagine a canyon floor,
cornstalks growing in rows
along a sunlit sandstone wall
        in the far corner of a room   late in life.

A field of moonlight
double-parked   in snowmelt
absorbs coyote fur
as it smokes through pincers
          disassembling heaving from breathing.

Capped with nesting swallows,
pollen clouds barb
the waning moon's tapered gown
to a crown of krill and sea-foam.

Amber clouds of bone marrow
lathered over corn husks—
are crushed sideways into a toothache,
where waning daylight's tongue-scent
          bleeds through a flypapered horizon.

One year before last—
I noticed a foot tied with horsehair
          in the shade of a cedar tree,
          horse milk dripping
          from the bullwhipped gavel near it.

I replace what I saw
        with what I heard,

pull out a letter
sent from *ourself* to my *selves*

—and for a second
        the flattened field is chandeliered
                by desert animal constellations.

This mountain stands near us: *mountaining,*
it mistakes morning for mourning
when we wear slippers of steam
      to erase our carbon footprint.

Wind's fingers wearing yours
you unravel a plow of harvested light,
notice its embers
      when scrubbed on drowned faces—

         repel fossilized wind.

The mind's wind
unlaces hammering
over pixelated heel bones
clasped to the nerve endings
of my fingers' ghosts.

These hands *glocked*
in a hive of red ants
swan through children
grunting at the bank
of one language
while the other
tethers moonlight to firelight—

their dark flitting
unthreads this land
from deveined searchlights
groping for embers in eyes
that blur while blinking.

How the map must look
when black water is ladled
        from white water.

When it's your face
        that ripples silver,
not mule deer skipping across
        the creek's forgetting.

How it might be then,
to look through silicone eyes,
see a worm's spigot maw
        dangling atop the periphery
        of an ax blade's slumber.

Blueing under a dimming North Star,
the Reservation's ghost
paws cartilage *pincered* from a digital cloud.

Its gnawed bones' opaque sigh—
the pallor of bleached wasp eggs—
throbs on tree knobs
        penciled in with burnt ivory smell.

Rising out of the uranium pond—
home picks: *bird flight*
from a cartouche box,
        it then becomes a chain of floating islands.

Slipping into free fall,
we drip-pattern: *the somewhere parts,*
our shoulders dissolving
                    in somewhere mud.

The arcing sun whistles
across the mask's abalone brow;
its blurring pouts into a forest
chirping from a lake's bite marks
stamped vertically on this map's windowsill.

Kneeling our thoughts on ellipses
evaporating from ollas of fragrant wet clay—
we saddle the drowning's slippery rim.

A hovering smear
trailing desert washes
fenced in with a murder of mirrors
        illumines the eating groaning over us.

Nibbling blades of winter light:
the goat's bleating leased downwind
pastures among foals dripping out
        of hollowed-out dictionaries.

Jeweled with houseflies,
leather rattles, foil wrapped,
ferment in beaked masks
        on the shores of evaporating lakes.

This plot, now a hotel garden,
its fountain gushing forth—
the slashed wrists of the Colorado.

To window the past:
        slide blurred eyes in.

To door the future:
        steam open ice-licked mice skulls,
        fling them against walls whitewashed
        until thinness surfaces, cooing.

A field that shivered with a thousand cranes

               evaporates in someone else's backyard.

Gills sliced into the mountain's crest   resin hourly.

Televised vapor muzzles a hummingbird's gassed lungs.

A cliff line wavers
             under a table's August.

Shears jangle in the corral's black-and-white photograph.

In the trailer's hallway: the night's unveiled ankles.

Rented from a shepherd of doves
      we return   replenished with categories.

We are husbands to razed hillsides, wives to drowned bridges.

When interred in plexiglass: our origin *salinated.*

Semicolons coughed out by the final raven
        sizzle the hand's parched memory.

Demagnetized moans drizzle magnetic north.

Unbelted, we plunge through our closed minds—open palmed.

The blowing sand of our faces' tongues
buried in the hovering;
the hovering buried twice
      and through the cage we swell
           new teeth throbbing in our lungs.

Bison-bone sled
crumbles where a sentry
piled feathered torsos
        —lit them on fire.

Dog-eared in amnesia: questions spear *what* to *why.*

Knotted to the gun's reflection,
        the storm, unknotting—
                the new *there*
                                thickening in thinning air.

Dimmest below our downward gaze—
                these stars gazing   back at us.

                How self-indulgent that moon—*always looking down.*

Unvaulted shadows varnish
        their ghosts' leaf patterns in unlit elevators.

What's left in their chests—
        scrapes teeth on bonemeal.

They pile ellipses on feathered gears
murmuring inside their coffins' pill-shaped whispers,
then trawl mountains
for bleached weather patterns
        clipped from view with body heat.

Somewhere a gun's shadow,
borrowed from their husbands' deaths,
        leaks the smell of desert rain.

Elsewhere—chemical burns
trail our brothers' sons
rifling alleyways for plates of coal dust
        bundled in factory-grown fur.

Everywhere is dreamed: *arranged.*

There's a way out—
walk the dirt road into cerulean dawn,
tap with clear fingerprints
the windows of cars and trucks
rattling down Highway 77,
and clasp the nine eyes of the desert
shut at the intersection of *then* and *now*.

Ask: will this whirlwind
connect to that one,
       making them cousins to the knife?

Will lake mist etched
on flakes of flood-birthed moonlight
hang its beard on a tow truck
hoisting up a buck,
       butterflies leaking from its nostrils,
       dark clouds draining off its cedar coat?

Mud-splattered thought patterns
sift into the stems of a sandpainting
of a tree of birds on a factory floor.
        It tethers the hill's nape
        to dry mouths
        rooting in shifting scree.

Silica-crusted gourds crackle
on the singed hides of gray mustangs
galloping through night's thinning hair.
        Its frayed hemline
        rims the street,
        when a left turns right   onto *clear.*

The camera sees a storm,
its eyes: bullet blasts
stacked atop
        gas-soaked magpie wings.

Ceramic ladles scrape snares
drinking our knees through our ankles.

Hyphens sash the tree line's dashes;
sleep seeps from its turquoise wails.

A lake, now a tire-rut pool,
leaves bitter aftertastes
on single-roomed tongues.

Doves, shrink-wrapped in brown skin,
swallow stiff voices
            atop the hum of closed envelopes.

A bottom-lit sea ponders the lake's questions,
their secret conversations
thatching howls to whimpers exhaled
from an isthmus of drowned wolves.

Its glossary's cataclysms
smoothed over the hatchet
tucked into a sheath of starlight
    locates fractures potted in cisterns of smog.

The stitching then unthreads
to muzzled worms pulsing
where an arsonist begins to lather heat over his neck.

Backlit by a caravan of wailing fathers
he silences their smeared faces
while kneeling in an arbor of mesh and steel.

    Nowhere streams in blips and beeps under them.

Benches face *before.*

I push into a coin slot:
        the sound of pills pebbling
        an emergency room floor.

          My thinking *stills.*

A new oxygen fills my reasons   for stalling.

Cranes pass as swans
    through tunnels underneath this dreaming,

                    I breathe it in.

Cave paintings stammering from their speech of clear water
    hoof this chamber quiet,

                    I breathe it in.

Charred cradles, tethered to anchors,
    molt beside bleached saddles,

                    I breathe it in.

The dark before me, unfolded from bead-pressed earth,
    sparkles, groans, whistles,

                    I breathe it in.

Exhaled knuckle dust
     calcifies a paralyzed wail.

Tossed out with bathwater, we sleep
     collared to our children's nooses.

Songs *feet* contemplation—
it bends a glimmer
     into a fishhook's winter shadow.

Swarming with cloud swell,
the land's swollen entrance
steams cuticles open to fevers
drying on dashboards.

Wave patterns shade the eyes of ants
from which we continue to watch:
moons, suns, nights,
pulled
     one pill at a time.

Ladders follow us from mines
in which our quivering
stretches hospital gowns
        into looms of lightning.

We shake ground deer hooves,
on the four directions of *forgive,*
while tire-lit flames grope
        the underside of a spiderweb's   webbed thinking.

Nearing sandbank,
gray hair bending out of it,
a witness witnessed—
        maps of jet fuel residue
        draining mosquito hum
                on the beginnings of our eyes.

Scratching for throat heat,
aging in our backs—
      pollen bursts the mind's fading tree line.

Smoking downwind, one pixel at a time,
gleaned from crane beak:
      embers glimpse body scent
          lathered over a door
          hammered to an exit.

Feather-wrapped mountains
unclutter veins to what remains   collapsed
before sparking fires
          where moonlight warms knuckles
                    wriggling in the slick throats of the drowning.

Drained atop their scatter—
                    our sniffed-at hair.

You pin porch lights to cage bars
painted with harbor air,
sip molten glass sweating
on an equinox too hot
        to pluck open with brittle teeth.

Beneath our hovering,
tasered smoke sinks
an oar's roots
into its mouth of ten years.

The mapping we spoke of
in the subway—
chest fat of sleep's self-portrait,
        neighs spasms onto songs
        braiding their highest leaves

        into our necklaces of smoke.

Radio waves groan
under ashen dragonflies
when you polish irradiated triggers
      with scalped hair.

Sage and creosote
coat the withers of spray-painted horses.
New suns sizzle from slits   in their golden flanks.

In our cornfields,
piled waist high,
swept from clan melt
then steeped in bear grease—
relocated hyphens pollinate
headaches with blurred visions.

Father's dying ceased
when he refunded this *ours*
for fused hands plaster-coated
        in a glottal stop's brief paralysis.

Pinpricked holes for eyes,
reversible teeth hemmed in copper thread,
polished brow bone swiveling
through trimmed hedges—
        he atrophies this aftermath,

                its highest frond withering on maps
                that dreamed our shadows waterlogged.

He then howls a constellation of anchors
flung at blue birds pausing midflight
where pewter wind
                creaks shut over a raft's hesitation.

He explains the sun,
not carried by horse
but a ceiling lamp
flickering on our computer screens.

Mother threw a platter
of blind spots on her son,
without knowing that bees
ached in her feet.

The beads of her breath
sank into his chest—
        he kept them five long years.

A tassel of singed hair cinched
around his wrists,
latchkeys soothing songbirds
in his pockets of fire—
he stains the night's rim
with sprigs of dry air
exiting fevering bodies
        cupped briefly by their itching.

She dabs clear his brow,
remembers syringes filled with lake mist,
wonders whether it was him
who strung teeth marks
                across her wrist the night before.

Together, they pace
the ravine's gauge nearing empty,
        step upon a pale horse
        lying on the earth's heat,
        legs upright in the cattle guard,
                butcher paper stretched taut over wiry ribs.

Its gasping sent them barreling
        back toward the awakened cornfield.

Somewhere, between,
        they leaped back into their bodies;
                they didn't recognize their own voices.

Her apparition ferries
  the flowers of their bruises back to the severing.

The bullwhip's knotted eye turns toward her and only her.

When fences come to suckle,
  where will her mind's legs carry her?

Moths mill about her feet's sleeping fountains.

Her throat's cave claims each son's song,
wears them like tiger's legs
      across nights striped and fanged.

How they stretch between moon and helium,
how they weave, tuned and plucked
      out of the sea's gassed maw.

How they uncover, with clear hands,
a handful of hushed hours
held like silver coins,
      where their eyes fail to shut   for the third time.

Tearing apart cloud names—
pierced fog commands:
douse the inferno's ribs
with opaque forgetting,
clip dawn from the book's dusk,
unfasten the song's empty auditorium
        over a garden of mute foals.

Tearing apart fog names—
pierced cloud sings:
let them shriek from their hinges;
let them slice their gills open
with flint knives,
and circle their ghosts
as frog-skinned antelope;
let them drag their legs over a trail
anchored to a ladder
that has soaked up blood
since land began crawling out of anthills.

This plate's shape is pawned for bread.

Paper lungs collapse on bird claws
              clacking on my sleeve's ash.

When they seed guns with powdered bone awls,
              who will be injured by such blue dark?

Brushfires graze upon a fleet of soft-footed elk.

Under them—a hush returns,
      sistering everybody's blood clots   to each other.

Always the swarm when we crest the story's hive.

Always smoke roosting among swallows nesting in cupped hands.

A chopping block's cobalt hum,
mothing braids of summer lightning,

lulls a hatchet's handle loose
then capsizes children

aiming their flint spines toward
steering wheels thawing in house fires.

Suckled by shadows, suckling their feet,
enrolled in a disappearing act,

they hand-stitch starless skies
to their temporary faces.

Their scraping is a smear facing another smear.
Their sky's blue veins are horses neighing through them.

Their dream of lightning   dreams.

The blurring heaves blue
as it breathes out
  sacks of black hair.

Their faces *mountaining*
a lake's closed book
glimpse smashed cairns
  sealed in lizard scales.

Their past lays bright eggs
when silence lathers dragnets
over their mothers' words
  for refrigerator light,
    moon rock, *escape.*

See how they shiver,
even when their arms
are shined to a high gloss,
and the dawn light
reveals their stone teeth,
glinting inside a tree's whimpering.

Shifting shape—they pinch shut
the keyhole of hunger's tollbooth,
then release chirping birds
from their detachable wrists.

We remember their footsteps
moored in glass jars
but forget flattened huts
spilling their scars
over the renaming of past landslides.

Their shouts flail
from empty school chairs
          to blurry visions at closing time.

The vowels of the starved
hang over the sequel of them;
they are what raven's claws would sound like
when unzipped from fallen apples.

Gathered in thirds of halves,
they drain spotlights
on police dogs barking
at their floating cages.

Forearms sliced with ladders—
the climb downward
          climbs up to greet them.

A phantom-arm feeling
      wants them to return their feet.

Falling from their cut hair:
      hearth sounds *sunlighting*
            the hallway back to then.

Will their torched names
      walk again as lake water?

Will they charge a fee
      to resharpen the horns
            of our dull speech?

West of dying—
they ask to sleep
        in one another's arms,
then unravel from buildings
weaving upright where bayonets
stab the sea for warmth.

Their coiled shadows *obsidian,*
as they lace ribbons
of cedar bark into black wind,
then stretch gauze wrap
over gates swelling open
from razors glinting
        in their palms' heat.

Their imagined tails bridled
with spit-soaked ash
striate liquid light
        to where the dissection begins.

Behind their mothers' maced skulls
they push lantern-lit compasses
into unmapped seasons
        —wing wind with red skin.

Their viscous tails thaw
our tongues' coastlines
when they strap dawn's first glint
to a weather of creaking chairs
so black boots
won't be captured on cameras
        sniffing their bruised masks.

Stained-glass splinters
in their creased mouths;
their fists among mirrors
growling inside other fists.

Pixelating through sorrel skin—
they silhouette teeth
nailing thick mud to thin mud,
     and sing our horses to sleep on
their bark blankets to incubate
       lightbulbs flickering in egg cartons.

They inhale the pond's shadow
       while kneeing our shoulders to roan scent.

An overcast of them,
scraped from the water's footsteps—
           cinder the bull's damp chest.

Absorbing liquid night through gilled feet,
they cackle from sand dunes—
        silver teeth twitching in their beaks.

Moans sip light from dilated pupils—
the seizure bids them to stay.

The elevator door shuts for the year
when they press their palms flat against
the fogged rim of the Reservation—

no sound steals past their squawking.

Reaching into their buckskin pouches,
they finger the patter of feet, loosened.

Foreheads torchlit,
they drift above hornet clouds, notice:
heaving under a corona of rearranged stars:
the People

wagering for more   more.

They *pronouned* dawning's expiration date with singed macaw feathers.

Suddenly they were this close   this far.

This hour, not the ridge, not their jumping-off point.

The sea drinking through them   hears the unraveling also.

The scraping of a train engine nearing childhood whimpers under them.

What lies beneath *naming:* they curl outward with wool scent.

Still, a noose glimmers above the orphaning field.

They forget to *forget* they were ours only during   the itching.

ACKNOWLEDGMENTS

Certain selections from *Dissolve* were published in *Black Renaissance Noire, Colorado Review, Kenyon Review Online, New England Review, Poetry, Waxwing, World Literature Today,* and *Yellow Medicine Review.*

My deepest gratitude to the Lannan Foundation, the Native Arts and Cultures Foundation, and the Norman Mailer Center for their generous support and resources that helped me complete this book.

Special thanks to Arthur Sze, Jon Davis, Sonja Kravanja, Orlando White, Ken White, Joan Naviyuk Kane, Allison Hedge Coke, Santee Frazier, and Ilya Kaminsky for looking at early versions of this work. Your feedback and generosity of spirit have been incredibly helpful. Extended gratitude to Joy Harjo, Luci Tapahonso, dg okpik, Sandra Alcosser, Debra Earling, Adrian Matejka, Bill Wetzel, Robyko; my colleagues and students in the low-residency MFA program at the Institute of American Indian Arts; and Michael Wiegers and everyone at Copper Canyon Press. Finally, ahéhee to Valaurie, my parents James and Earlene, my siblings, and my nieces and nephew, whose caring support makes my work possible. I want to also acknowledge my extended family: the Bįįhbitoonii Tódich'ii'nii of Bidaázi'géé, the Tł'ízíłání of Tiistsooznááti, the Maiideezgizhnii of Tsezhintcho'í, and the Nakaidiné of Tzézhinsikléé'.

ABOUT THE AUTHOR

Sherwin Bitsui was raised in White Cone, Arizona, on the Navajo Reservation. He is the author of three collections of poetry, including *Flood Song,* which won an American Book Award in 2010. He is a winner of the Whiting Award and has served on the faculty of the Institute of American Indian Arts since 2013.

Lannan Literary Selections

For two decades Lannan Foundation has supported the publication and distribution of exceptional literary works. Copper Canyon Press gratefully acknowledges their support.

LANNAN LITERARY SELECTIONS 2018

Sherwin Bitsui, *Dissolve*

Jenny George, *The Dream of Reason*

Ha Jin, *A Distant Center*

Aimee Nezhukumatathil, *Oceanic*

C.D. Wright, *Casting Deep Shade*

RECENT LANNAN LITERARY SELECTIONS FROM
COPPER CANYON PRESS

Josh Bell, *Alamo Theory*

Marianne Boruch, *Cadaver, Speak*

Olena Kalytiak Davis, *The Poem She Didn't Write and Other Poems*

Michael Dickman, *Green Migraine*

John Freeman, *Maps*

Deborah Landau, *The Uses of the Body*

Maurice Manning, *One Man's Dark*

Rachel McKibbens, *blud*

W.S. Merwin, *The Lice*

Camille Rankine, *Incorrect Merciful Impulses*

Roger Reeves, *King Me*

Paisley Rekdal, *Imaginary Vessels*

Brenda Shaughnessy, *So Much Synth*

Richard Siken, *War of the Foxes*

Frank Stanford, *What About This: Collected Poems of Frank Stanford*

Ocean Vuong, *Night Sky with Exit Wounds*

Javier Zamora, *Unaccompanied*

Ghassan Zaqtan (translated by Fady Joudah), *The Silence That Remains*

Poetry is vital to language and living. Since 1972, Copper Canyon Press has published extraordinary poetry from around the world to engage the imaginations and intellects of readers, writers, booksellers, librarians, teachers, students, and donors.

WE ARE GRATEFUL FOR THE MAJOR SUPPORT PROVIDED BY:

THE PAUL G. ALLEN
FAMILY FOUNDATION

Anonymous

Jill Baker and Jeffrey Bishop

Anne and Geoff Barker

Donna and Matt Bellew

John Branch

Diana Broze

Sarah and Tim Cavanaugh

Beatrice R. and Joseph A. Coleman Foundation

Laurie and Oskar Eustis

Mimi Gardner Gates

Linda Gerrard and Walter Parsons

Nancy Gifford

Gull Industries Inc.
on behalf of Ruth and William True

The Trust of Warren A. Gummow

Phil Kovacevich and Eric Wechsler

Lakeside Industries Inc.
on behalf of Jeanne Marie Lee

TO LEARN MORE ABOUT UNDERWRITING
COPPER CANYON PRESS TITLES,
PLEASE CALL 360-385-4925 EXT. 103

WE ARE GRATEFUL FOR THE MAJOR SUPPORT PROVIDED BY:

Maureen Lee and Mark Busto
Rhoady Lee and Alan Gartenhaus
Ellie Mathews and Carl Youngmann as The North Press
Anne O'Donnell and John Phillips
Petunia Charitable Fund and adviser Elizabeth Hebert
Gay Phinney
Suzie Rapp and Mark Hamilton
Emily and Dan Raymond
Jill and Bill Ruckelshaus
Kim and Jeff Seely
Richard Swank
University Research Council of DePaul University
Vincentian Endowment Foundation
Dan Waggoner
Barbara and Charles Wright
Caleb Young and Keep It Cinematic
The dedicated interns and faithful volunteers
of Copper Canyon Press

The Chinese character for poetry is made up of two parts:
"word" and "temple." It also serves as pressmark for
Copper Canyon Press.

This book is set in Parable, designed by Christopher Burke, with display
headings set in Sanuk Big, designed by Xavier Dupré. Book design by
VJB/Scribe. Printed on archival-quality paper.